FAIRGROUND

presents

BONNIE & CLYDE

by Adam Peck

BONNIE & CLYDE

by **Adam Peck**

Performers
Catherine McKinnon
Eoin Slattery

Written by Adam Peck
Directed by Tid
Composition, lyrics and sound design by Peter Swaffer-Reynolds
Designed by Chris Gylee
Lighting designed by Matthew Graham

Assistant director – Emily Thompson
Assistant producer – Eleanor Fogg
Assistant designer – Ruby Spencer
Assistant stage manager – Jesse Meadows
Costume supervisor – Corina Bona
Costume maker – Eleanor Condon
Scenic artist – Philippa Thomas

FAIRGROUND was founded in 2007 by Tid and Adam to make theatre that is epic in subject and scope, and combines original scripts, new musical compositions and highly physical performance. The creative team works collaboratively to make intelligent, exciting and visually engaging theatre.

Artistic Director
Tid

Co-Founders
Tid and Adam Peck

Creative Team
Matt Graham, Chris Gylee, Catherine McKinnon,
Adam Peck, Peter Reynolds, Tid

DIRECTOR'S NOTES ON BONNIE & CLYDE

All stories to which we connect are, in some way, about us: about our relationships, our needs and desires, the pains and pleasures of being human. When I thought about making *Bonnie & Clyde* with Adam, I was driven by very simple things: by the idea that these two people did something extraordinary, that they were in love, and that they wanted something more from life. When I was growing up I wanted more too – I didn't want to be poor, lonely or ordinary – and that is what attracted me to this story.

In making this show as a company we have shared words, songs, thoughts and ideas, and we have imagined ourselves as other people – as Bonnie and Clyde. We have researched their lives and in the specific details of their stories we have found things that are important to us. And that is what theatre is about. It is born out of our need to share our experiences of the world – to relate to and connect with other people – in an attempt to affirm our lives through our stories. And so to that end, I believe that theatre belongs to everyone, and as our stories are passed from one person to another theatre becomes not only a means of communication, but a record of our existence and a celebration of who we are.

Catherine McKinnon (Bonnie)
Trained at The Oxford School of Drama.
For Fairground: *Out of Touch – A Trilogy*, *The Red Man*
Theatre: *Antony & Cleopatra* and *Julius Caesar* (Shakespeare at the Tobacco
Factory), *20,000 Leagues Under The Office* (Publick Transport, Tour)

Eoin Slattery (Clyde)
Trained at the Bristol Old Vic Theatre School.
Theatre: *The Adventures of Pinocchio* (Tobacco Factory), *Rum & Vodka*
(Corner Boy, National tour), *Women on the Verge of HRT* (Nick Brooke,
National tour), *Eddie King's Unforgettable Tour…* (Tobacco Factory),
Guildenstern in Hamlet (Cork Opera House), *Faust is Dead* (Samuel Beckett
Theatre, Dublin), *The Trial of Jesus* (Corcadorca).TV & Film: *Borstal Boy*
(Hell's Kitchen), *Casualty* (BBC), *Eye for an Eye* (RTE).

Adam Peck (Writer)
Adam is a playwright and actor, and teaches a weekly playwriting course
for young people at the Bristol Old Vic. He has a degree in Theatre and
Performance Studies from Warwick University, and an MA in Theatre
(Playwriting) from Royal Holloway University.
Writing credits:
For Fairground: *Out of Touch – A Trilogy*, *The Red Man*, *Where You Can't Follow*.
My Bristol Vista (Paines Plough), *Chocolate Money* (Short Fuses, Bristol
Old Vic), *Kick-Off* (Ferment, Bristol Old Vic), *Joan of Arc* and *Gilgamesh*
(Bristol Old Vic Young Company).
Acting credits:
For Fairground: *Out of Touch – A Trilogy*, *The Red Man*, *Where You Can't Follow*.
Theatre: *My Bristol Vista* (Bristol Old Vic).

Tid (Director)
Tid is a director and actor, and Artistic Director of Fairground. He
trained at East 15 Acting School (where he received the Henry Cotton
Award for Acting), and then went on to work and train with Lecoq-based
theatre company, Pants on Fire. Tid was recently Movement Director
on Tom Morris's *Juliet and her Romeo* at Bristol Old Vic, and is currently
working on a new theatrical endeavour named The Ensemble.
Directing credits:
For Fairground: *Out of Touch – A Trilogy*, *The Red Man*, *Where You Can't Follow*.
For Rough Cut: *Stitched*, *Four Ladders*, *Okeanos*.
For Bristol Old Vic Young Company: *Jason and Medea*, *Two*, *The Leaving*,
Brave, *Let Me Hear You Dance*, *Samson and Delilah*, *Roberto Zucco Narcissus and
Echo*, *Other Worlds*, *Joan of Arc*, *Romeo and Juliet*, *Blood Wedding*, *Masque of the Red
Death*, *Gilgamesh*, *Mountain Language*.

Acting credits:
For Rough Cut: *A Collection of Incredible Stories* (Oxford House), *Stitched* (Edinburgh Fringe Festival).
For Pants On Fire: *Splice* (Edinburgh Fringe Festival), *Tossed! - The Tempest* (People Show Studios), *Narciss I* (Chisenhale Dance Space), *The Tale of Rancor* (New York Fringe Festival and Philadelphia Fringe Festival).
Film: *Narcissus* (Salon Films UK).
Writing credits for Bristol Old Vic Young Company: *Jason and Medea*, *Samson and Delilah* (co-writer), *Narcissus and Echo*.
www.visitfairground.co.uk

Chris Gylee (Designer)
Trained at the Bristol Old Vic Theatre School.
For Fairground: *Out of Touch – A Trilogy*, *The Red Man*.
Oliver Twist (the egg), *Colörs*, *Tattoo* (Company of Angels), *Henry V* (Southwark Playhouse), *Shooting Rats* (Fanshen), *Hamlet*, *The Taming of the Shrew*, *Othello*, *Much Ado About Nothing* (Shakespeare at the Tobacco Factory).
www.chrisgylee.co.uk

Peter Swaffer-Reynolds (Composer, Lyricist and Sound Designer)
In 2005 Peter began working with Tid at the Bristol Old Vic. They have worked together since then. When Fairground was formed he was invited to be collaborative partner and has produced the music for all their shows. His primary years were spent in Scandinavia. He has worked for Welsh National Opera, National Theatre of Wales, Moon Fool Theatre, Green Ginger and NoFitState Circus. Circus has inspired everything – it is one of the most beautiful things he knows.

Matthew Graham (Lighting Designer)
Trained at Royal Welsh College of Music and Drama.
For Tobacco Factory Theatre: *The Adventures of Pinocchio*, *Ali Baba*, *A Christmas Carol*, *Alice Through The Looking Glass*; *Tosca*, *Carmen* and *Rigoletto* (Opera Project). *Jason and Medea* (Bristol Old Vic), *Ugly Duckling* (Traveling Light), *Blue Orange* (Plain Clothes Theatre Company), *Muzzle* (Jonny Dixon), *Macbeth*, *Twelfth Night*, *The Tempest*, *Love/ Intrigue*, *Robbers* (Faction Theatre Company), *Babel in Italy* (Élan Productions), *Odette*, *Coriolanus*, *Closer Than Ever* and *Medea* (Guidecca Productions).

Emily Thompson (Assistant Director)

Emily is a theatre practitioner specialising in physical, collaborative, and devised performance. She is currently based in London, and in her final year of studying for a BA in English and Drama at Royal Holloway University. Her career began as part of the Bristol Old Vic Young Company where she worked with Tid; her professional debut coming in 2008, in Fairground's production of *The Red Man*. Emily also practices as a freelance facilitator for young performers, working as an Associate Artist for the Bristol Old Vic Young Company, and most recently for the National Youth Theatre of Great Britain. The performer as actor, musician, and dramaturg is important to her, as is the role of the director within the collaborative creative process.

Acting credits:

For Fairground: *The Red Man*.

For Bristol Old Vic Young Company: *Roberto Zucco, Narcissus and Echo, Joan of Arc, Blood Wedding*. Film: *Swarm* (Twisted Theatre).

Assistant director credits: *Out of Touch – A Trilogy, Samson and Delilah* (Co-writer).

Eleanor Fogg (Assistant Producer)

Assistant Producer: *Swallows and Amazons* (Bristol Old Vic).

Assistant Director: *Faith Healer* (Bristol Old Vic).

Producer & Director: *One Day I Said No* and *So Lonesome I Could Cry* (Desperate Men). I enjoy both making my own work, and supporting others whose work I admire.

Ruby Spencer (Assistant Designer)

Ruby is currently working as the costume supervisor on Bristol Old Vic's production of *Faith Healer*, and is planning to go to university in 2011 to study Theatre Design. She has worked with Bristol Old Vic Young Company since she was six years old, gaining experience as an actor, director, deviser, choreographer and designer. Her most recent credits include designer for *Jason and Medea* and assistant designer for *Two* (Bristol Old Vic Young Company); Assistant Director for *Fallen* (Bristol Old Vic Young Company and Bristol Harbour Festival); and as an actor in the Bristol Old Vic Young Company's production of *Our Country's Good* which won an award at the National Student Drama Festival, 2010.

Jesse Meadows (Assistant Stage Manager)

Jesse is a Bristol-based theatre practitioner. Having graduated in 2010 with a first class honours degree in Theatre and Performance from Warwick University, she is now applying her skills in performance and production to the vibrant Bristol theatre scene. She began her career with the Bristol Old Vic Young Company, and has gone on to work with professional theatre companies, including Fail Better Productions and Fairground. Jesse is currently a member of 'Made in Bristol' at Bristol Old Vic, where she also assists Young Company workshops. She is looking to develop her career as a performer and theatre maker.

Acting credits: *Three Women* (Warwick Student Arts Festival), *Persephone* and *Play Without a Title* (Fail Better Productions), *The Skriker* (National Student Drama Festival, 2008), *Blood Wedding* (Bristol Old Vic Young Company), *Through the Wire* (Tobacco Factory).

Producer credits: *Jason and Medea* (Bristol Old Vic Young Company), *By the Bog of Cats* (Warwick Arts Centre Studio, National Student Drama Festival, 2009 & 2010).

Assistant Producer: *Pedestrian* (Underbelly, Edinburgh Fringe Festival), *Diary of a Madman* (Fail Better Productions).

Adam Peck

BONNIE & CLYDE

OBERON BOOKS
LONDON

First published in 2011 by Oberon Books Ltd
521 Caledonian Road, London N7 9RH
Tel: 020 7607 3637 / Fax: 020 7607 3629
e-mail: info@oberonbooks.com
www.oberonbooks.com

Excerpt on page 15 is reproduced from Timothy Egan's *The
Worst Hard Time: The Untold Story of Those Who Survived the Great
American Dust Bowl* (Houghton Mifflin, 2006).

A catalogue record for this book is available from the British
Library.

ISBN: 978-1-84943-123-1

Cover image: © Andreas Gradin / istockphoto.com

Printed in Great Britain by CPI Antony Rowe, Chippenham.

AUTHOR'S NOTES

A shift. indicates a shift in mode, mood, space, time etc. It should be interpreted as you see fit.

Bonnie and Clyde have Texan accents. To this end:

- the letter 'g' has been omitted from most words normally ending in 'ing'.
- the word 'of' has been replaced by the letter 'a', in some instances as a suffix, in others as a separate word.
- the word 'you' appears in the script as both 'you' and 'ya' depending on the context.

However, pronunciation of all words should be as you see fit.

I have tried to apostrophise as few words as possible to facilitate reading/performance.

I am hugely indebted to Jeff Guinn for his excellent biography of Bonnie and Clyde, _Go Down Together: The True, Untold Story of Bonnie and Clyde_ – it was an invaluable resource to both myself and the creative team behind the original production.

With thanks to Morgan Matthews, Ali Robertson, Emma Stenning, Mary and Geoff Peck, Kate Yedigaroff, Sharon Clark, and all at Tobacco Factory Theatre.

With special thanks to the people who were involved in the workshops and discussions that took place before and during the writing process – you know who you are.

Characters

BONNIE PARKER

CLYDE BARROW

Bonnie & Clyde was first performed on 5th October 2010, at The Brewery, Tobacco Factory Theatre, Bristol. It transferred to Theatre 503, London on 18th January 2011.

BONNIE, Catherine McKinnon
CLYDE, Eoin Slattery

Written by Adam Peck
Directed by Tid
Composition, lyrics and sound design by Peter Swaffer-Reynolds
Designed by Chris Gylee
Lighting designed by Matthew Graham
Assistant director – Emily Thompson
Assistant producer – Eleanor Fogg
Assistant designer – Ruby Spencer
Assistant stage manager – Jesse Meadows
Costume supervisor – Corina Bona
Costume maker – Eleanor Condon
Scenic artist – Philippa Thomas

Produced by FAIRGROUND

May 1932.

A disused barn in an unnamed southern state of the United States of America.

BONNIE and CLYDE look out.

BONNIE & CLYDE   We humbly acknowledge there is a time to live, and a time to die. *(Beat.)* For the gift of life, we are grateful. *(Beat.)* You have breathed into us the breath of existence – given us the minds and bodies in which we now live. *(Beat.)* For this place in which we temporarily dwell, for the devotion that continues to unite us, for the peace bequeathed to us this day, we thank you.

Pause.

We have not allowed ourselves to become victims. We have decided our own destiny. We have chosen to live lives less ordinary.

A shift.

BONNIE picks up a newspaper and reads out loud.

BONNIE   We have done what no hailstorm, no blizzard, no tornado, no drought, no epic siege of frost, no prairie fire, nothing in the natural history of the southern plains has ever done. We have stripped the land so bare, removed the grass so completely, that these thirty-three million acres of land will never be the same again. *(Beat.)* These 10,000 foot high black blizzards are encasin bodies with whirlin sand, flailin

> skin with edges like steel wool, fillin lungs
> with enough grit to make it feel as though
> we have already drawn our last gasp of air.

BONNIE stops reading.

> They sure as hell got that right.
>
> Clyde, are you listenin to me? *(Beat.)*
> Daddy?

CLYDE   What is it?

BONNIE   You listenin to me?

CLYDE   Sure I am… Just thinkin's all.

BONNIE   Everythin alright…?

CLYDE   Everythin's fine.

BONNIE   Well why don't ya come sit with me?

CLYDE   Cos I don't wanna come sit with ya.

BONNIE   Fine. I'll just sit here on my own then.

CLYDE   Fine.

BONNIE   Fine, I will. But I sure would like it if you'd
           listen to me when I'm talkin to ya.

CLYDE   I thought you was readin the paper…

BONNIE   I *was* readin the paper. I was readin the
           paper *to you.*

CLYDE   Right. Well maybe next time ya can give
           me a bit a warnin.

BONNIE	Next time I won't bother.
CLYDE	Fine.
BONNIE	Fine.

Long Pause.

	Ya thought about maybe just spendin some time together? Ya thought a that…?
CLYDE	We *are* spendin time together.
BONNIE	Oh we are…! Forgive me for not noticin.
CLYDE	I'm thinkin is all!
BONNIE	Sure y'are – you've been *thinkin* all day! What about me?
CLYDE	You got somethin important to say?! Go ahead say it. But all I'm hearin's prattlin. *(Beat.)* If I wanted to know the news I'd ask, or else I'd read it myself, alright?! *(Beat.)* So are ya gonna shut up, or ya got somethin to say?
BONNIE	No.

Beat.

CLYDE	Good. I'm havin a wash.

CLYDE goes outside and washes, tending to a bullet wound on his shoulder. BONNIE tends to her damaged leg, removing old bandages, cutting new ones, etc.

BONNIE	*(Shouting outside.)* Daddy?

CLYDE	What is it?
BONNIE	Could ya bring me a bowl for my leg when you're done?
CLYDE	A what?
BONNIE	Some water… for my leg.
CLYDE	Sure… It hurtin?
BONNIE	No more than normal.
CLYDE	Ya been takin the morphine like I said?
BONNIE	I have.
CLYDE	Good girl.

Long Pause.

BONNIE	That shoulder a yours alright?
CLYDE	Looking fine.

CLYDE comes back inside with a bowl of water, which he gives to BONNIE.

	Sure is deep though – gonna take some time to mend.
BONNIE	Anythin I can do?
CLYDE	Maybe some a that ointment…
BONNIE	Come on then.

BONNIE takes a swab with some ointment, and cleans CLYDE's shoulder.
He winces with pain.

CLYDE   God damn! Be careful!

BONNIE   I am bein careful.

A shift.

CLYDE   Tomorrow we wake up late. We're runnin
                         late. And things just ain't feelin right. The
                         air's warm and muggy. The sun's strugglin
                         to break through the blanket a dusty
                         clouds. Our heads are full a thoughts,
                         mainly about the past. But we don't say
                         much. We've said most things already. So
                         even though we're motorin into the future,
                         it don't feel like there's nothin much to
                         look forward to no more.

Beat.

                         The highway runs west between Gibsland
                         and Mount Lebanon, then gradually
                         curves south and into a dirt track that
                         throws the car and us from side to side.
                         We're pushin 60, and the clock's showin
                         9.13 – not so bad considerin we slept so
                         late. To the left a low green carpet a bean
                         plants. To the right a wall a thick wooded
                         greenery. A fence on either side separatin
                         the rough from the road. Straight up ahead
                         a truck pulled up full a chickens bound for
                         the slaughterhouse. I wonder if they know
                         where they're headin.

A shift.

BONNIE	Why didn't ya kill that boy yesterday?
CLYDE	Cos he had his whole life ahead a him.
BONNIE	He was shoutin so loud, he couldda got us both killed…
CLYDE	Well he didn't and everyone's doin just fine now aren't they…?
BONNIE	You've got a big heart when it comes to killin…
CLYDE	Most people ain't choosin to be in the firin line. *(Beat.)* That boy was just scared. And fear ain't no reason to die.

Pause.

	He had a kind look in his eye – like he never meant to harm nobody.
BONNIE	Is that how you used to look Clyde…? Before ya started doin this?
CLYDE	I don't remember how I looked.

CLYDE lies down.

BONNIE goes outside.

<u>*A shift.*</u>

BONNIE	Fairgrounds, ferris wheels and photo booths. Dressin up, meetin up, and makin out. *(Beat.)* Bright coloured flowers. Fluffy white clouds. People laughin and whoopin,

goofin around. *(Beat.)* My name lit up in electric lights. Momma on the front row, proud. Admirers by the stage door, waitin for autographs. Floor to ceilin mirrors, Maybelline make-up, and a dressin table fit for a star. It's showtime for Bonnie Parker! Bonnie Parker, it's showtime!

A shift.

(From outside.) Where's my mouse?

CLYDE	I killed him.

BONNIE hurries back inside, carrying a small box.

BONNIE	You did not?!
CLYDE	No, I did.
BONNIE	Why?
CLYDE	He was gettin real noisy – squeakin and scratchin – I could hear him through the wall.
BONNIE	So ya killed him?
CLYDE	Slit his throat!
BONNIE	How could you?
CLYDE	Pretty easy. Wasn't like I didn't know where to find him.
BONNIE	He never did nothin to nobody.
CLYDE	So why d'ya keep him prisoner?

BONNIE	He was a friend.
CLYDE	I wouldn't keep no friend a mine in a box – not unless he owed me money.
BONNIE	I don't believe you. *(Beat.)* Where is he?

CLYDE rubs his tummy.

CLYDE	Mighty tasty he was. Wouldda been better with some peas and cream, but still…
BONNIE	You ate him?!
CLYDE	Yeah. Put him in a sandwich. Tasted good.
BONNIE	When? I've been here the whole time…
CLYDE	You was havin a wash.
BONNIE	I don't believe you.
CLYDE	I cooked him on the fire.
BONNIE	You ain't killed him – I can tell.
CLYDE	What makes ya so sure?
BONNIE	You wouldn't do that… Clyde…? *(Beat.)* Ya killed him?!
CLYDE	I told ya I did.
BONNIE	You killed our mouse?!

BONNIE picks up a gun and points it at CLYDE. CLYDE is unmoved.

CLYDE	I wouldda said 'your mouse'. I had very little to do with him… besides the killin, I mean.
BONNIE	That's one a the worst things you've ever done.
CLYDE	Glad ya think so – makes me feel a whole lot better about the other things.
BONNIE	Ya know I talked to him – he kept me company.
CLYDE	Was a bit one way friendship wouldn't ya say?

BONNIE goes closer to him with the gun.

BONNIE	Tell me he ain't dead.
CLYDE	Ya want me to lie to ya?
BONNIE	No. I want ya to tell me he ain't dead.
CLYDE	Alright – he ain't dead.
BONNIE	You didn't eat him?
CLYDE	I didn't eat him.
BONNIE	You let him go… cos ya felt sorry for him.
CLYDE	Cos I felt sorry for him.
BONNIE	Good.

BONNIE lowers the gun.

CLYDE	Good.
BONNIE	That's alright then.
CLYDE	That's alright then.
BONNIE	Stop that.
CLYDE	Stop that.
BONNIE	I mean it.
CLYDE	I mean it.

BONNIE lifts the gun again.

BONNIE	I'll kill you!
CLYDE	I'll kill you!
BONNIE	Childish…
CLYDE	Childish…
BONNIE	You are!
CLYDE	You are!

Pause.

There ain't no bullets in that gun by the way.

BONNIE throws the gun at CLYDE and goes outside with the box. She lights a fire in a pan, and burns the box.

BONNIE   We shall wipe away the tears from our eyes
And there shall be no more death

Neither sorrow, nor cryin.
Neither shall there be any more pain,
For all those things are passed away.

CLYDE   *(Loudly.)* Amen!

BONNIE comes back inside. She deliberately does not make eye-contact with CLYDE.

Pause.

I didn't kill him… *(Beat.)* I opened the lid to have a look at him, and he took one look at me like he'd licked a donkey's ass and left.

BONNIE   I don't blame him.

CLYDE   Me neither – I'd run away from me.

Long Pause.

Where would you rather live – in a house that spread out over an acre, but was only one storey high… or at the top of a tower that had thousands a storeys, but only one room on each storey?

BONNIE   Well, there ain't much to look at in Texas, so there's no point bein up high. And it sure sounds like a lot a effort gettin up and down.

CLYDE   If ya was high up you could see if the laws was comin…

BONNIE   Couldn't make a quick getaway though…
                  No, I think I'd like all those different
                  interconnectin rooms – like a maze, that
                  only we'd know the way around. Lots a
                  rooms – a quiet lounge with a sofa and
                  a piano – friends in one wing, family in
                  another. A table for playin pool… a pool
                  for swimmin in – like a big hotel full a
                  everythin we wanted.

CLYDE   A pool sure would be nice. *(Beat.)* Now
                  you do one for me…

BONNIE   Alright. *(Beat.)* What would you rather be
                  – a zebra with fadin stripes, or a horse with
                  stripes comin up? No wait… I got a better
                  one. A zebra with stripes that you could
                  see for miles around, like they was lit up,
                  or a sandy coloured horse that blended
                  into the background, like it was invisible?

CLYDE   Oh, that's good! *(Beat.)* Well I like the idea
                  of everyone lookin at me, wonderin how
                  my stripes light up. But it sure would be
                  nice to blend into the background…

BONNIE   So which would you be?

CLYDE   I'd be fifty fifty.

BONNIE   No you can't. Anyway, what'd be the point
                  a that?

CLYDE   I'd have my head and shoulders sandy
                  so if I was facin ya, I'd be invisible… but
                  my body all stripey so when I ran away
                  people'd know who I was. They'd say,

26

"we just got duped by that stripey invisible zebra horse. He's one of a kind that one".

BONNIE   No, that ain't allowed – you gotta choose.

CLYDE   Alright. Considerin our line a work, I'd go invisible.

Pause.

Ya like it here?

BONNIE   I miss home.

CLYDE   You miss The Bog?!

BONNIE   The people I mean. *(Beat.)* You think they're proud of us?

CLYDE   Sure they are – they're the same as us. Just they're stuck in their daily grind. I bet they're lookin at us thinkin, 'If I had the gumption, I'd be doin exactly the same as you – robbin from the rich'.

BONNIE   Is that what we're doin…?

CLYDE   That's exactly what we're doin. Labourin for a dollar a day ain't workin for nobody. Nobody except the rich – cos they got the system all set up in their favour. I tell ya, we fought one war to gain our independence, and now there's another – between those who've got a lot more than what they deserve and those who deserve a lot more than what they got.

BONNIE	You should run for President talkin like that!
CLYDE	Maybe I will.
BONNIE	You'd be good at tellin other people what to do.
CLYDE	I'd make the right decisions.
BONNIE	That'd make a change… for the President I mean. *(Beat.)* How's about somethin for dinner?
CLYDE	What we got's in the trunk. But you callin it dinner's the biggest overstatement I ever heard.
BONNIE	I'm havin sardines.
CLYDE	You'll turn into a sardine if ya carry on eatin them the way y'are.
BONNIE	I like 'em.
CLYDE	I noticed. I'll go take a look.

Beat.

BONNIE	Daddy?
CLYDE	Yeah…
BONNIE	Ya won't leave me will ya?
CLYDE	I won't.
BONNIE	I mean ever…

CLYDE   I mean ever too. *(Beat.)* I'll be right back.

CLYDE goes outside.

A shift.

BONNIE   Why d'ya look at me that way last time we
                         were home? You ain't ever looked at me
                         like that before. *(Beat.)* I think you've seen
                         the end of us… comin real soon. I'm glad
                         ya didn't say so if you have. You got a way
                         with those sorts a things.

Pause.

                         What if we've already said goodbye and
                         not even noticed. What if I never see you
                         again – I'd be real sad if that were true.

Pause.

                         Clyde says we're gonna go somewhere
                         new tomorrow. Where we gonna go…?
                         Another barn? Another sleepless night
                         in the back of a car, too scared to light a
                         candle or a fire to warm ourselves? We're
                         not goin anywhere. Sometimes I wonder if
                         we've ever gone anywhere at all.

A shift.

CLYDE returns with tins of food and begins preparing for 'dinner'.

CLYDE   I am likin that car a lot! 'Specially the
                         colour. Cordoba Grey's what Mr Ford's
                         called it. Now don't that sound like the
                         greatest colour?

BONNIE	Cordoba Grey.
CLYDE	Even feels good in your mouth when ya say it! Cordoba Grey.
BONNIE	Cordoba Grey. You're right – feels real good.
CLYDE	Thing is, it ain't even grey! Reflects like it's brown or orange, sometimes even red. I wonder how they do that… Sure is somethin special.
BONNIE	I do like it when ya get excited about your cars.
CLYDE	Remember that letter I wrote to Mr Ford tellin him what a good V8 he makes?
BONNIE	Course I do, I told ya what to write.
CLYDE	You did not tell me what to write!
BONNIE	I helped ya then.
CLYDE	More like it… Ya think he got it?
BONNIE	Why wouldn't he? It's not like we got the wrong address. *(Shouting.)* We know where you live Mr Ford!
CLYDE	That's somethin I couldda done honey – worked on all those mighty fine automobiles. And I wouldda been good at it too. Cos I wouldda cared about it. Doin somethin that's worth somethin. *(Beat.)* Think how far people're gonna travel in

the future, with these machines they're developin… Sure is somethin I couldda gotten my teeth stuck into…

BONNIE   You couldda done anythin you wanted…

CLYDE   If they'da let me.

Beat.

BONNIE   Robbin banks ain't all that bad!

CLYDE   S'pose it requires a little more brain power than what I wouldda been doin – fittin windows or makin pies. And it sure as hell beats workin hard your whole damn life, for nothin.

Beat.

BONNIE   There wasn't any sardines?

CLYDE   You must've eaten 'em all.

BONNIE   So what we got?

CLYDE   Ham or beans. Or we can go fifty-fifty…?

BONNIE   Fifty-fifty.

A shift.

CLYDE   The growlin engine, the air rushin in through the open winda, the dry dirt flickin up from the road – drownin out the silence that would otherwise have been. She turns to speak, says nothing. I look the other way, pretendin I haven't noticed – stare at the low sky. A black bird's up high, glidin, riding the warm air, trackin our journey from here to there. His silhouetted head nods toward me, and I nod back. We both know what's comin. *(Beat.)* She turns on the radio and it's playin our song. She smiles, starts singin again.

A shift.

BONNIE and CLYDE eat the ham and beans.

BONNIE	Do ya think Jesus knows what we're doin…?
CLYDE	I don't think Jesus knows what anyone's doin – he's dead.
BONNIE	My momma'd slap you for sayin that…
CLYDE	I'm sure she would. She'd slap the hind off a donkey for neighin.
BONNIE	She's a good woman and you know it.
CLYDE	Funny way a showin it.
BONNIE	Clyde…!
CLYDE	You've seen the way she looks at me – all narrow-eyed and nasty.
BONNIE	That's my momma you're talkin about!
CLYDE	Like I'm evil or somethin.

BONNIE	She just wants what's best for me.
CLYDE	I'm sure she does. Don't mean she has to hate on me though!
BONNIE	She don't hate on ya.
CLYDE	Course she does. *(Beat.)* She disliked me before she even knew me!
BONNIE	Maybe she's got a sixth sense…
CLYDE	For what?
BONNIE	Trouble.
CLYDE	Trouble…?!
BONNIE	But I like trouble myself.

Pause.

CLYDE	Did she like Roy?
BONNIE	What?! No!
CLYDE	No what?
BONNIE	Just no.
CLYDE	So she did like him?
BONNIE	Things was different back then. I was happier.
CLYDE	I thought you said you were never happy?

BONNIE   I don't mean happier. I mean hopeful… like somethin good might come my way.

CLYDE   And did it?

BONNIE   It sure did – Clyde Barrow came my way, and he got my heart pumpin real fast!

CLYDE   That's nice honey. But what about Roy?

BONNIE   What about him?!

CLYDE   Did he get your heart pumpin fast?

BONNIE   No he did not! *(Beat.)* Why d'ya wanna talk about Roy all of a sudden?

CLYDE   Just came to mind is all…

BONNIE   Well ya can put it outta ya mind. Why don't we talk about you and Eleanor Bee Williams! How d'ya like that?

CLYDE   That's completely different – I didn't give her no ring.

BONNIE   I was young…

CLYDE   You were married!

BONNIE   Still am! Don't mean nothin!

CLYDE   So why d'ya still wear it?

BONNIE   It's the only gold I got.

Beat.

CLYDE	Did he used to kiss that tattoo on your thigh?
BONNIE	Clyde!
CLYDE	Well did he? Did he put his head between your legs?
BONNIE	I don't wanna talk about this.
CLYDE	Tell me, I don't care.
BONNIE	Well why ya askin?
CLYDE	Cos I wanna know.
BONNIE	Well I don't wanna tell.
CLYDE	Why don't ya just level with me about Roy?!
BONNIE	Cos it's not important!
CLYDE	Important enough for ya to still wear his ring! And ya wouldn'ta got the tattoo *there*, if there was nothin going on...
BONNIE	I got it *there* cos I didn't want my momma to see, okay! *(Beat.)* You happy now – you and your sordid mind?!

Pause.

	I don't understand you Clyde, I really don't... It's like ya don't want us to have a nice time.
CLYDE	I do want us to have a nice time.

35

BONNIE   Well what's Roy got to do with anythin?

CLYDE   Just wonderin why your momma liked him
               and not me.

BONNIE   She didn't like him! He just never got me
               into any trouble.

CLYDE   Neither have I!

BONNIE   You know what I mean… He did his thing
               – whatever that was… and left me to do
               mine.

CLYDE   Oh, I've dragged ya along against your will
               now have I?

BONNIE   Things just sortta… presented themselves
               with you.

CLYDE   Choices ya mean?

BONNIE   Yeah…

CLYDE   So why don't she see it that way?

BONNIE   You know what moms are like.

Beat.

CLYDE   I think you've said somethin to her!

BONNIE   Like what?

CLYDE   I dunno – paintin me in a bad light…

BONNIE   That's an awful thing to say!

CLYDE   Well have ya?!

BONNIE   No I have not!

CLYDE   You're lyin!

BONNIE   Why would I do that?

CLYDE   Cos ya wanna keep things… separate.

BONNIE   Alright, next time we're home I'll tell her
            – in front of you, so you know I've done
            it – I'll tell her that I'm here a my own
            volition.

CLYDE   Good – stop her from lookin at me the way
            she does…

BONNIE   S'not gonna change nothin though. She
            just always had high hopes for me!

CLYDE   Higher than a boy from The Devil's Back
            Porch…?

BONNIE   She thought I might get me the attentions
            of an oil man or somethin.

CLYDE   An oil man! S'pose you got the looks.

BONNIE   What's that s'posed to mean?

CLYDE   You know what it means.

BONNIE   But I didn't want no oil man. I wanted
            Clyde Barrow to come whisk me off my
            feet! And he sure as hell did that! My very
            own Billy the Kid!

CLYDE   Jesse James if ya don't mind!

Pause.

                 What would you a done if I hadn'ta come
                 by?

BONNIE   Been famous…

CLYDE   Oh yeah…?! Doin what – servin coffee
                 and turnin tricks?

BONNIE   No! Singin and dancin!

CLYDE   Oh I forgot ya had a meetin with destiny
                 planned!

BONNIE   You know I knew I'd be famous!

CLYDE   And how exactly were you gonna trade in
                 servitude for stardom?

BONNIE   I don't know, but I was…!

CLYDE   Cos I'm not sure how Broadway fits in
                 with sellin hot flesh.

Beat.

BONNIE   Why are you bein mean to me?

CLYDE   I'm not.

BONNIE   I wanted to save enough money for a ticket
                 to New York.

CLYDE   I wanted to earn an honest livin… What ya
                 want don't mean nothin.

BONNIE	Well *I am* famous! You can't deny that!
CLYDE	True – but only cossa me!

Pause.

Bet you never thought you'd be doin this…

BONNIE	Sure did not! *(Sarcastically.)* Ham and beans is all I ever wished for. Not to mention the five-star accommodation…!
CLYDE	If ya don't like it, I can drop ya home…
BONNIE	Sure thing – when we gonna go?
CLYDE	Now if ya like.
BONNIE	*(Standing.)* Alright, come on then.

BONNIE goes to walk away. CLYDE grabs her and pulls her back.

CLYDE	I like you Bonnie Parker.
BONNIE	Why ya sayin that now?
CLYDE	Cos I do like ya. I just get frustrated is all. *(Beat.)* But when I look in those eyes –
BONNIE	*Those eyes*?! Maybe ya should look in *those eyes* a little more often – I got things goin on in there you should take a look at!

A shift.

CLYDE	The chicken coup on wheels still ain't movin and it's blockin our path. I squeeze my foot on the brake, roll the wheel

towards the field a corn, bring the car to a halt. The green rustles to the left – we both look with tired eyes but there's nothin to see – prob'ly a rock rollin from the road or a wild animal runnin away… The car's idlin by the side a the road. I look at her lookin pretty, eatin her breakfast, bright blonde hair fallin over her shoulders. I open the door, my foot resting on the runnin board, and there it is again, the rustlin in the green.

A shift.

BONNIE   Do you find me attractive Clyde… as a woman I mean?

CLYDE   Course I do.

BONNIE   Just ya don't… ya know… touch me like ya used to.

CLYDE   I can touch ya.

BONNIE   Well why don't ya then?

CLYDE   Well I will.

BONNIE   Now?

CLYDE   If that's what ya want…?

BONNIE   I'd like that…

CLYDE   Well I will.

CLYDE puts his hand up BONNIE's skirt and touches her. She enjoys it, but then she sees that CLYDE has closed his eyes.

BONNIE   Why have ya shut your eyes?

CLYDE   Dunno.

Beat.

BONNIE   Are you thinkin a someone else?

CLYDE   No!

BONNIE   I don't want ya to do it with your eyes shut.

CLYDE   Alright, I won't.

CLYDE touches BONNIE again.

                Do ya like that?

BONNIE   Yeah.

CLYDE   Does that feel good?

BONNIE   Yeah. Feels real good.

BONNIE takes CLYDE's hand further.

                Oh that's it. That's right. *(Beat.)* Oh, faster… Faster!

CLYDE   I don't need tellin what to do.

They continue.

BONNIE   That's right. That's it. Oh…

CLYDE pulls away just as BONNIE is about to orgasm.

CLYDE   I can't do this!

CLYDE gets up and goes outside. He washes his hands.

<u>*A shift.*</u>

> An icy breeze brushes the top a my head, and a darker cloud throws shadow over the valley. The black bird swoops and perches on the top a the truck, like it's mockin the chickens imprisoned inside. Somethin's wrong. I half turn my body back through the open door. She's leanin across, eyes wide open, sayin, shoutin somethin I can't make out. I've barely moved when I hear the first shot.

<u>*A shift.*</u>

CLYDE returns. He takes a bundle of clothes from a bag and throws them on the floor. He then takes out a tin of peaches which he opens and begins to eat.

BONNIE   *(Referring to the clothes.)* What's all that?

CLYDE   Some a them fancy clothes.

BONNIE looks through the clothes, enjoying the feel of the fabrics. She picks out a pair of heeled shoes, then a dress which she holds up to show CLYDE.

BONNIE   Oh this is real pretty…!

CLYDE ignores her.

BONNIE picks out a pair of stockings and begins to put them on.

CLYDE spots the tattoo on her leg.

CLYDE   Why ain't ya ever got a tattoo with my
                 name on it…?

BONNIE   I don't believe it! *(Beat.)* I got bullet-
                 holes and a gammy leg for ya – ain't that
                 enough?

CLYDE   S'pose when ya put it like that…

BONNIE   You jealous?

CLYDE   No.

BONNIE   That's alright then.

BONNIE continues to dress-up.

                 Sure is nice not havin Boodles around…

CLYDE   Ya don't like Boodles now?

BONNIE   Just good to get some privacy.

CLYDE   We couldda done another job today if he'd
                 a been around.

BONNIE   I know, but it's nice just the two of us… No
                 Buck or Blanche.

CLYDE   I'd a preferred Buck here than dead!

BONNIE   I know. But like ya said yourself – we
                 all got it comin – just some sooner than
                 others.

Pause.

	When we go, we'll be lyin side by side for eternity…
CLYDE	Don't start that again.
BONNIE	What?
CLYDE	You know full well what!
BONNIE	Well we will won't we?! We'll be lying next to each other you and I – you promised.
CLYDE	I did no such thing.
BONNIE	You did too.
CLYDE	On the contrary – I promised my momma I'd go in with Buck.
BONNIE	I see.
CLYDE	You know that is what happened, so don't do this!
BONNIE	Do what?
CLYDE	The sad eyes and the soft voice routine. *(Beat.)* Last time we were in Dallas she told us both – you were there – that she'd left the gravestone blank so she can get both our names engraved at the same time.
BONNIE	Well that is real charmin – wishin away her own son!

CLYDE   She knows we're not gonna last forever out here, doin what we're doin.

BONNIE   Plannin for death's hardly helpin.

CLYDE   It's cheaper – and I don't blame her for that.

BONNIE   How come I don't remember this?

CLYDE   Cos you were drunk. Or else you're lyin now to get me to talk about it.

BONNIE   More like ya were whisperin behind my back. *(Beat.)* Did ya whisper about where my dead body's gonna go?

CLYDE   You'll be in with the Parker's...

BONNIE   I don't wanna be in with the Parker's – I wanna be with you.

CLYDE   I don't think we got much say in the matter.

BONNIE   We got rights!

CLYDE   Ya think people're gonna care about our rights?

BONNIE   I'm gonna write me a will – and yours too – tellin everyone what we want!

CLYDE   You'll do no such thing!

BONNIE   Why not?!

CLYDE   Cos I don't want ya to!

BONNIE	Cos ya don't wanna be next to me, d'ya?! *(Beat.)* I knew it! I knew ya didn't care about me!
CLYDE	Don't get all hissy about this. When you're dead you're not gonna know whether I'm lyin next to ya or not!
BONNIE	As in life!
CLYDE	What?!

Beat.

BONNIE	I said, as in life!
CLYDE	You'd better take that back…
BONNIE	I will not.
CLYDE	No? *(Beat.)* D'ya want me to hit ya?
BONNIE	Yeah I do.
CLYDE	I will.
BONNIE	I know ya will.

Beat.

Go on then. Then ya can start cryin on the floor, feelin all sorry for yourself.

CLYDE grabs BONNIE by the throat.

CLYDE	You've got an evil vein in you.
BONNIE	You and me both!

BONNIE spits in his face and pulls away.

CLYDE chases her and goes to grab her.

BONNIE turns and draws a gun.

> I'll shoot ya! Don't think I won't.

CLYDE   Oh yeah?! Then what ya gonna do?

BONNIE   Bury ya – just where I want ya.

CLYDE   Oh yeah!

BONNIE   Yeah! Then I'm gonna get in the grave and kill myself. Won't be goin anywhere then will ya – with me lyin on top a ya?! And Momma Barrow can go shoot!

CLYDE   Give me that!

CLYDE grabs the gun from BONNIE.

> You are one stupid girl sometimes. What ya doin wavin that in my face?!

BONNIE   I just want ya to listen to me!

CLYDE   I am listenin to ya!

BONNIE   You never listen to nobody. Ya never listened to Buck or Blanche, and look what happened to them!

CLYDE   Those things are not my fault!

BONNIE   Whose *fault* are they then?

CLYDE   People made their choices.

BONNIE   And my leg – whose *fault* is that?

CLYDE   You're still alive cossa me!

BONNIE   I'm nearly dead cossa you. And all I want
               is for you to love me!

CLYDE   I do love ya!

BONNIE   Just not enough…!

Beat.

CLYDE   When I go my momma'll a seen two a her
               sons die before she does! And that ain't
               right. So I'm goin in the ground next to
               Buck. I owe her that at least.

BONNIE screams and starts crying.

CLYDE ignores her and sits down.

<u>*A shift.*</u>

               The bullet of a Remington Model 8
               rifle deflects off the frame between the
               windshield and the driver's door. Another
               soon follows through the open winda,
               passes through the car and ricochets off the
               fence on her side. *(Beat.)* It's the third that
               I don't see or hear. The third that hits me
               on the left temple, just in front a my ear,
               ploughs through my head and exits outta
               the other side a my skull. But I can see
               what happens next.

A shift.

BONNIE   Will ya talk to her about me goin in with
                  the Barrows?

CLYDE   I'll talk to her. But what's your momma
                  gonna say?

BONNIE   I've written her a letter, tellin her what I
                  want. She'll understand.

                  (Beat.) So you'll talk to her?

CLYDE   I said I will.

BONNIE   Ya promise?

CLYDE   I promise.

BONNIE   Ya promise, ya promise?

CLYDE   I promise, I promise.

Pause.

BONNIE   Ya don't have to pretend, ya know…?

CLYDE   I know.

BONNIE   Ya don't have to make like everythin's fine
                  to try and make me feel better. Ya know
                  that don't ya?

CLYDE   Yeah.

BONNIE   That's alright then.

Pause.

BONNIE takes out a newspaper.

	We're in the paper again.
CLYDE	Oh yeah...?
BONNIE	The one I picked up in Shreveport...
CLYDE	Why didn't ya say?
BONNIE	I didn't think ya deserved it.
CLYDE	Well thank you! *(Beat.)* Any pictures?
BONNIE	I wanna read ya the story first. *(Beat.)* It's about a robbery in Sherman.
CLYDE	But we ain't been to Texas in weeks!
BONNIE	We were there Friday accordin to this.
CLYDE	Anybody hurt?
BONNIE	I'm guessing so by the headline. "Barrow Gang Slaughters Butcher".
CLYDE	Where do these people get off, pinnin these things on us?!!
BONNIE	They gotta blame somebody...
CLYDE	Well I don't like it!
BONNIE	Bad publicity's better than none.
CLYDE	Not when it comes to killin it ain't.
BONNIE	Shall I read ya what it says...?

CLYDE   Go on.

BONNIE   *(Reading.)* Yesterday mornin, shortly before
               6 o'clock, a lone gunman, thought to be
               the infamous Clyde Barrow, entered the
               convenience store between Dickson Street
               and the Square, demandin the contents a
               the till. When the store-keeper, a Mr James
               T Taylor appeared to hesitate, the gunman
               raised his revolver and warned –

CLYDE casually play-acts the people BONNIE describes.

CLYDE   "Hurry up or you'll get it."

BONNIE   At that moment the shop's butcher, a Mr
               Homer Glaze, entered the store from a
               back room, saying to Barrow –

CLYDE   "You can't do that son. Now get outta
               here."

BONNIE   Barrow turned quickly, his mean little eyes
               snappin… *(Stops reading, turns to CLYDE.)*
               You haven't got mean eyes baby. *(Reading
               again.)* …now pointin his gun at Glaze and
               replied –

CLYDE   "I can't, can I?"

BONNIE   Followed by a blast a gunfire. As Glaze fell
               with Barrow's bullet in his heart, Taylor
               ran towards the dyin man, only to be
               warned –

CLYDE   "Get back, or I'll give you some a the
               same."

BONNIE   Barrow then fired three more bullets
                into the butcher, before runnin from the
                store and into the back of a black sedan.
                Motorin off at high speed in the direction a
                the Oklahoma state border, the pair were
                heard shoutin –

CLYDE   "Eat my dust suckers! Yee-hah."

BONNIE   Officers failed to pursue.

BONNIE stops reading.

                Now that sure is somethin to be proud of!

CLYDE   Why?

BONNIE   What d'ya mean 'why'?

CLYDE   They killed an unarmed man, left with
                nothin!

BONNIE   It made the papers!

CLYDE   So what? That paper's celebratin idiocy.

BONNIE   It's things like this has made you as feared
                as Jesse James – people is as scared a you
                as they ever were a him.

CLYDE   I never meant to kill nobody…

BONNIE   I know, but people get in the way don't
                they…?

CLYDE   These small-timers are shootin people
                willy-nilly – they ain't got no purpose.

BONNIE	Some might say this man Glaze deserved it – he stuck his nose in where it wasn't wanted and he got shot. But that store-keeper, well, he knew what was good for him, and he's still alive. And that there's a lesson for everybody. *(Beat.)* Wanna see the picture?
CLYDE	I don't like my name on other people's wrong-doin's.
BONNIE	You're looking mighty fine…
CLYDE	*(Taking the paper.)* Let me see that. *(He looks.)* Not so bad.
BONNIE	I got another one from Grapevine. Wanna see?
CLYDE	Grapevine…?! Where ya been hidin that?
BONNIE	Never you mind! There's bound to be somethin real in this one.
CLYDE	After I've eaten.
BONNIE	Oh come on, it'll only take a minute.
CLYDE	I ain't too proud a what we done in Grapevine.
BONNIE	Boodles just misunderstood what ya was sayin…
CLYDE	And two men ended up dead. Stupid!

BONNIE   'Death's part a what we do' – ain't that
                what ya used to say? *(Beat.)* At least it was
                the laws that died and no-one else.

CLYDE   S'pose.

Beat.

BONNIE   Why are we still doin this, if you're so
                ashamed all of a sudden…?

CLYDE   I'm not ashamed – just not so fond a death.

BONNIE   Since when?

CLYDE   Since now.

A shift.

                My eyes bulge and the veins on my
                forehead rise like somethin's boilin inside
                a me. Blood runs outta my nose, down my
                chin, and stains my Blue Western dress
                shirt. Through the hole in my face ya can
                see my teeth… clenched together, like
                a snarlin dog. My lifeless body lurches
                forward and my shattered head slips
                through the spokes a the steerin wheel.

A shift.

CLYDE continues eating his peaches.

BONNIE takes out another newspaper and reads to herself.

Pause.

BONNIE	Oh Clyde, I think we done somethin real bad this time.
CLYDE	What is it?
BONNIE	This poor girl Marie Tullis. We killed her fiancé last week. *(Beat.)* Those two bikers… one of them was her fiancé.
CLYDE	That's a real shame honey.
BONNIE	Is that all ya got to say?
CLYDE	What else d'ya want?
BONNIE	Look at her! Look at her face! She's lookin real sad cossa what we done.
CLYDE	I'm lookin real sad cossa what lotsa people've done.
BONNIE	Look at her. Wearin her weddin dress to the funeral…
CLYDE	I don't wanna look.
BONNIE	No, I bet ya don't.
CLYDE	What's the good in lookin? Don't change nothin.
BONNIE	She was nineteen…
CLYDE	Well she's got time to get another man then hasn't she…?

BONNIE	People ya love are not replaceable. *(Beat.)* Is that what you'd do if I died – just get someone else?
CLYDE	No.

Long Pause.

BONNIE	We could get married for them…
CLYDE	What you talkin about…?
BONNIE	You know… pretend like we is gettin married. I got that pretty little dress I could wear, and those heels…
CLYDE	And what would be the point a that?
BONNIE	I dunno. Might make us feel better. Like release somethin or somethin. You know, they might be lookin down at us, and realise that we're not so bad after all. That we never meant to do what we did. *(Beat.)* It's worth a try.
CLYDE	And what exactly are we gonna be tryin to do?
BONNIE	I dunno… Forgive ourselves… Let them see that we're not bad people.
CLYDE	We are bad people.
BONNIE	No we're not.

Pause.

	Oh come on… Might be fun…
CLYDE	Alright. Alright. But if you're wearin a dress I wanna look nice too.
BONNIE	Ya do look nice.
CLYDE	I mean properly – suit and tie and all that!
BONNIE	Well come on then.

BONNIE and CLYDE find suitable 'wedding clothes' from the bag and floor, and begin to change.

CLYDE	So, what do we say?
BONNIE	I do.
CLYDE	And that's it?
BONNIE	That's the important part.
CLYDE	'I do' what?
BONNIE	Take thee to be my lawfully wedded wife.
CLYDE	Right.
BONNIE	In sickness, in health, for richer, for poorer, till death us do part. Amen.

Pause.

	You look nice.
CLYDE	I know.

Pause.

BONNIE   I wanna do your tie.

CLYDE   Come on then.

BONNIE finishes getting dressed and ties CLYDE's necktie.

BONNIE   Over. Over. Under and through.

BONNIE fastens the knot.

CLYDE   Not too tight.

CLYDE loosens the knot.

BONNIE removes her ring.

BONNIE   We can use this as the ring.

CLYDE   I don't wanna use that.

BONNIE   We won't have rings then!

CLYDE   Fine.

BONNIE   Fine. *(Beat.)* Right. Do the words…

CLYDE   I take thee Bonnie Parker to be my lawfully wedded wife.

BONNIE   That's it… And the rest…

CLYDE   You just said the rest.

BONNIE   I did, but you gotta do it too.

CLYDE   Why?

BONNIE	Cos that's how it goes. Come on – in sickness.
CLYDE	In sickness.
BONNIE	In health.
CLYDE	In health.
BONNIE	For richer.
CLYDE	For richer.
BONNIE	For poorer.
CLYDE	For poorer.
BONNIE	Till death us do part.
CLYDE	Till death us do part.

BONNIE and CLYDE kiss.

A shift.

She has just enough time to see I'm dead
and that she'll soon be joinin. She screams
a high shrill while her body jumps up
and down like a rag-doll – two in the
thigh, one in the knee, fifteen more in her
shoulders and arms. The car's perforated,
rockin from side to side with slug after slug
from the gunmen's guns, blood and flesh
splattered inside and out. Cordoba grey
turned red. She's riddled with bullets, but
none enough to finish it. Then a merciful
one hits her in the mouth, tearin her lip

from the rest of her face, exits through the top of her spine and she's gone too.

Pause.

BONNIE   Ya gonna carry me across the threshold?

CLYDE   If that's what ya want.

BONNIE   I want.

CLYDE picks up BONNIE in a deliberately clumsy way.

BONNIE   Properly.

CLYDE   I am doin it properly.

CLYDE readjusts so he has BONNIE 'properly' in his arms, then carries her outside.

BONNIE   Careful a my leg!

CLYDE carries BONNIE back inside and puts her down on the bed. BONNIE looks at CLYDE expectantly, but CLYDE turns away. BONNIE is disappointed.

                What would ya rather be... a tiny bird
                with pretty little wings... that flies as fast
                as lightnin? Or... a giant eagle that could
                only fly – ?

CLYDE   Giant eagle.

BONNIE   Wait! I haven't finished...

CLYDE   I don't care what else you're gonna say
                – I'd be the eagle.

BONNIE	I knew you'd say that.
CLYDE	You'd be the tiny bird wouldn't ya?
BONNIE	I would.
CLYDE	I could carry you around in my talons.
BONNIE	Not too tight.
CLYDE	Then maybe I'd eat ya.
BONNIE	You would not eat me!
CLYDE	Or just peck at your head when I'm hungry.
BONNIE	You could do that. I'd let ya do that.
CLYDE	I can do whatever I want – I'm the golden eagle.
BONNIE	Until someone shoots ya down.
CLYDE	I'd be too quick and too high for anyone to shoot me down.
BONNIE	I bet you would. You'd be the greatest eagle that ever lived.

Long Pause.

	What *would* ya do if I died and you didn't?
CLYDE	That ain't gonna happen.
BONNIE	But what if it did?

CLYDE	I'd kill myself.
BONNIE	How? What if there was nothin to kill yourself with?
CLYDE	I'd find a way.
BONNIE	What if they take your shoe laces and your belt… and there ain't no windows to break and no high places to jump from. What then?
CLYDE	I'd torment someone until they'd have to throttle me to death. Or I'd run head first into the wall until I was all mangled and brain-damaged.
BONNIE	You'd do that for me?
CLYDE	I sure would.

Beat.

BONNIE	What if there was no walls and no-one around?
CLYDE	I'd hold my breath.
BONNIE	That's impossible!
CLYDE	Not if I put my mind to it.
BONNIE	Alright, show me.

CLYDE takes a gasp of air and holds his breath.

A shift.

BONNIE and CLYDE foresee their own deaths.

CLYDE suddenly succumbs to breathing again.

BONNIE laughs.

	See. You can't do it!
CLYDE	That's cos I don't wanna do it. Why would I wanna die while you're still here?
BONNIE	That is so romantic.

Long Pause.

CLYDE	Shall I tell ya the end a the story now?
BONNIE	Is it gonna be as sad as the rest?
CLYDE	Afraid so.

Beat.

BONNIE	Alright...
CLYDE	You sure?
BONNIE	I'm sure.
CLYDE	Ya sure, ya sure?
BONNIE	I'm sure, I'm sure.
CLYDE	Alright.

A shift.

CLYDE speaks directly to BONNIE.

CLYDE   A cloud a smoke lingers over the car, like
          a mist, shroudin their handywork. There's
          laughin and jokin, someone's goofin
          around – like an echo – like a thought
          lands and our souls are spirited away.
          (Beat.) They're still firin their guns as they
          step closer to the car. They're watchin
          us ridin their lead – our bodies briefly
          revived by bullets, our blood paintin the
          leather interior. *(Beat.)* They peer inside,
          their hands restin on buckled metal and
          broken glass. They tip their hats to a job
          well done, then walk away. The truck
          starts up, the black bird takes flight and the
          squawking chickens fade into the distance.

*BONNIE and CLYDE remove their 'wedding clothes' and prepare for bed,
closing shutters and organising their clothes and guns for the following
day. They lay down together as if to go to sleep. BONNIE keeps her eyes
open and stares out front.*

BONNIE   We shall wipe away the tears from our eyes
          And there shall be no more death
          Neither sorrow, nor cryin.
          Neither shall there be any more pain,
          For all those things, with our passin away,
          are passed away.

Lights very, very slowly fade to black.